SABOTAGE & Silhouettes

Rashida Basaria

A Molding Messengers Publication

Sabotage & Silhouettes
Copyright © 2022 by Rashida Basaria

All rights reserved. Printed in the United States of America. No part of this book may be used or reproduced in any manner whatsoever without written permission except in the case of brief quotations embodied in critical articles or reviews.
This book is a work of fiction. Names, characters, businesses, organizations, places, events and incidents either are the product of the author's imagination or are used fictitiously. Any resemblance to actual persons, living or dead, events, or locales is entirely coincidental.

For information about permission to reproduce selections from this book, Write to Molding Messengers, LLC 1728 NE Miami Gardens Dr, Suite #111, North Miami Beach, FL, 33179 or email Info.Staff@MoldingMessengers.com
www.MoldingMessengers.com

Library of Congress Control Number: 2022902351
Print ISBN: 978-0-578-37153-5
eBook ISBN: 978-0-578-37154-2

A Molding Messengers Publication

SABOTAGE & *Silhouettes*

Rashida Basaria

A Molding Messengers Publication

Table of Contents

Acknowledgments IX

Introduction XIII

Chapter 1: Silhouettes 1

    Prayer 2

    Son (Takari) 3

    Silhouette 4

    Soulmate 5

    Destined 7

    I Deserve Love 8

    Second Chance 9

    Drunk Text 10

    Turn It Up 11

    Happy Hour 12

Chapter 2: Sacrifice 15

    The "Talking" Stage 16

    Love language 17

    Patient With Me 19

    You Give Me Butterflies 20

The Kinda Love	21
Love Showers	23
The One	26
Milk in His Coffee	28
How to Love You	30
Patiently	31
Red Flags	32
No, Thank You	35
You've Got a Hold on Me	37
First Time	39
Home	41
Cupid	42
Remy Straight	43
For the Streets	44
Lipstick Stains	46
The Other Woman	48
Am I?	50
It's Over	52
Raw	53
Love him	55
Never Lasts	57

Untitled 59

Fantasy 62

Chapter 3: Sabotage 65

Still Birth 66

Suicide Attempts 68

Myself 70

Rain 72

You Don't Wanna Love me 74

Breaking Point 76

Was It Worth It? 78

What If 79

Learning to Love 81

'Til Death 83

Loss for Words 85

Tainted 87

Slipping Away 89

Self-Destructive 90

Self-Sabotage 92

Discernment 94

Toxic 95

Insensitive 97

Triggered 99

Surviving 101

Smashed Art 103

Send Nudes 105

Chapter 4: Soul 107

Flower 108

Irrelevant 109

Words for Thought 111

Talent 113

Elevate 114

Epitome of a Gentleman 115

Save You 117

Transition 118

Stars Align 119

Pour Into You 120

Let Go 121

ACKNOWLEDGMENTS

Writing this book took a physical, emotional, and spiritual toll on me. Each poem is a part of me; something I had to go through to grow. I express myself best through my writing, and many do not know this. I spent countless hours and a massive number of tears pouring into this book. It was an enlightening and healing process that launched me into a spiritual rebirth. I hope it helps heal anyone who can relate or is/has gone through anything remotely resemblant of my trials and tribulations. I thank you for reading.

My most important 'thank you' goes to my son, Takari. You are my strength, my courage, my motivation. I love you more than life itself. Without you, none of this even matters. You have watched me laugh, cry, and struggle through finishing this book and I appreciate your support and patience with me as your mom. You've been through so much in your little 11 years and have watched me go through so many changes in our journey through this life. You are so brave and so strong, smart, funny, handsome, and amazing, and I am forever grateful for you.

A special thanks to my friends that have always supported me and been there for me, even through their own life challenges. Kimle, Helen, Brea, Tracey, Kimmy, Chana, Roosevelt, Grace, Ketsia, Jason, Melyssa, Christian, Javeste, Chuck, Quise. My family, Rafiq and Leah, my nephews Aiden, AJ, and James. You all have played a huge role in my growth and healing. If I didn't mention you, and you supported me in any way, shape, or form, thank you. I appreciate even the smallest things and words from each of you. All the support from my online followers who don't even know me in real life, I am beyond grateful for you all "seeing me".

Thank you to my mom, my brother Kat. I pray you both are resting in peace and watching over me. I hope I made you both proud.

To my daughter, Takai. I'm sorry we never got to meet, but you grew in me for 6 long months. I love you and I know you were too good for this world. Until we are reunited.

To the strangers of my past, I am forever grateful. Without you, a lot of these pieces wouldn't have been possible. I am thankful for every obstacle, every tragedy, every essential moment in my life. It has changed me and molded me into the person I am today.

And to those of my future, thank you in advance. You just may inspire my next book.

And a special thank you to God, and the Universe. This has been a long time coming and without my faith and the alignment of the stars, none of it would be possible.

I would also like to thank Jax and the entire Molding Messengers team for not only a stress-free and seamless process, but for providing a platform for first-time authors like myself to have an opportunity to publish and gain exposure. Their professionalism and encouragement along the way is unmatched. I am unfathomably grateful. Thank you

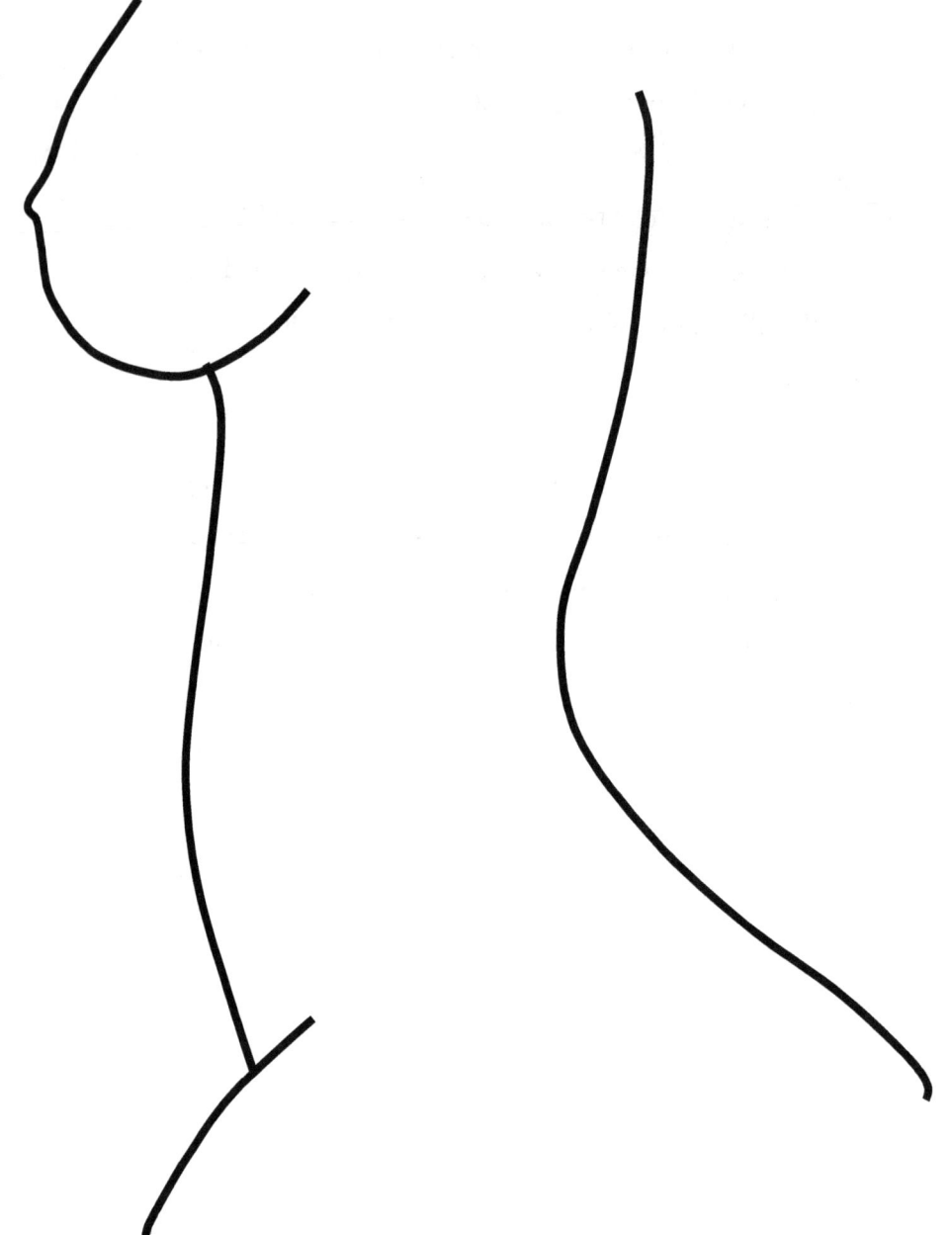

XII

INTRODUCTION

sab·o·tage
/ˈsabəˌtäZH/

verb
    1. deliberately destroy, damage, or obstruct (something), especially for political or military advantage.

Noun
    1. the action of sabotaging something.
       "a coordinated campaign of sabotage"

sil·hou·ette
/ˌsilooˈet/

noun
    1. the dark shape and outline of someone or something visible against a lighter background, especially in dim light.

Verb
    1. cast or show (someone or something) as a dark shape and outline against a lighter background.

Sabotage and Silhouettes has a deeper meaning that just two words thrown together to form a creative alliteration. Each word holds a significant meaning in the title of this book.

Sabotage is the deliberate damage, destruction, or obstruction of something. In this instance, it relates to my life, and possibly even parts of yours. The traumas that we go through, lead us to specific actions and emotions. When we feed into those emotions, we start to create chaos, sometimes intentionally and sometimes, unintentionally. Either way, we begin to self-sabotage. Whether we sabotage potential or existing relationships, important friendships, or even our own growth. We start to get in our own way. Many times, after the many losses I've gone through, I found myself sabotaging the very things that were sent to heal me.

Silhouettes are dark shapes or outlines of someone or something against a lighter background. Our dark parts. Especially in times of anguish or hardship. Through traumas, everything goes dark. The silhouettes represent the dark parts of our lives, our mentality, our soul. Even with light all around, a silhouette will remain dark, and the details are impossible to make out. This is exactly how I felt through all my dark times. I wasn't myself for months, maybe even a year or so, but the silhouettes hid the details in the dark while the light was still shining all around me. It made it hard for people to 'see' me. And even harder for me to 'show' myself to those around me. I shut down. And everything became dark.

Through these poems, I expose the darkness. I open myself up to the world. To be vulnerable, honest, and to speak my truth. Some of the hardest words I have ever had to write are in this book. We are all human and we all experience things. These pieces are just a part of my story.

WARNING

This book references suicide and may be triggering for some. Some of the content is extremely traumatic and explicit. If mentions of suicide or the details of death are triggers for you, please do not continue reading. Thank you for your support in purchasing this book. If you have thoughts of suicide or harming yourself or others, please call the National Suicide Prevention Hotline at 1-800-273-8255.

There is help. You are loved. You are enough.

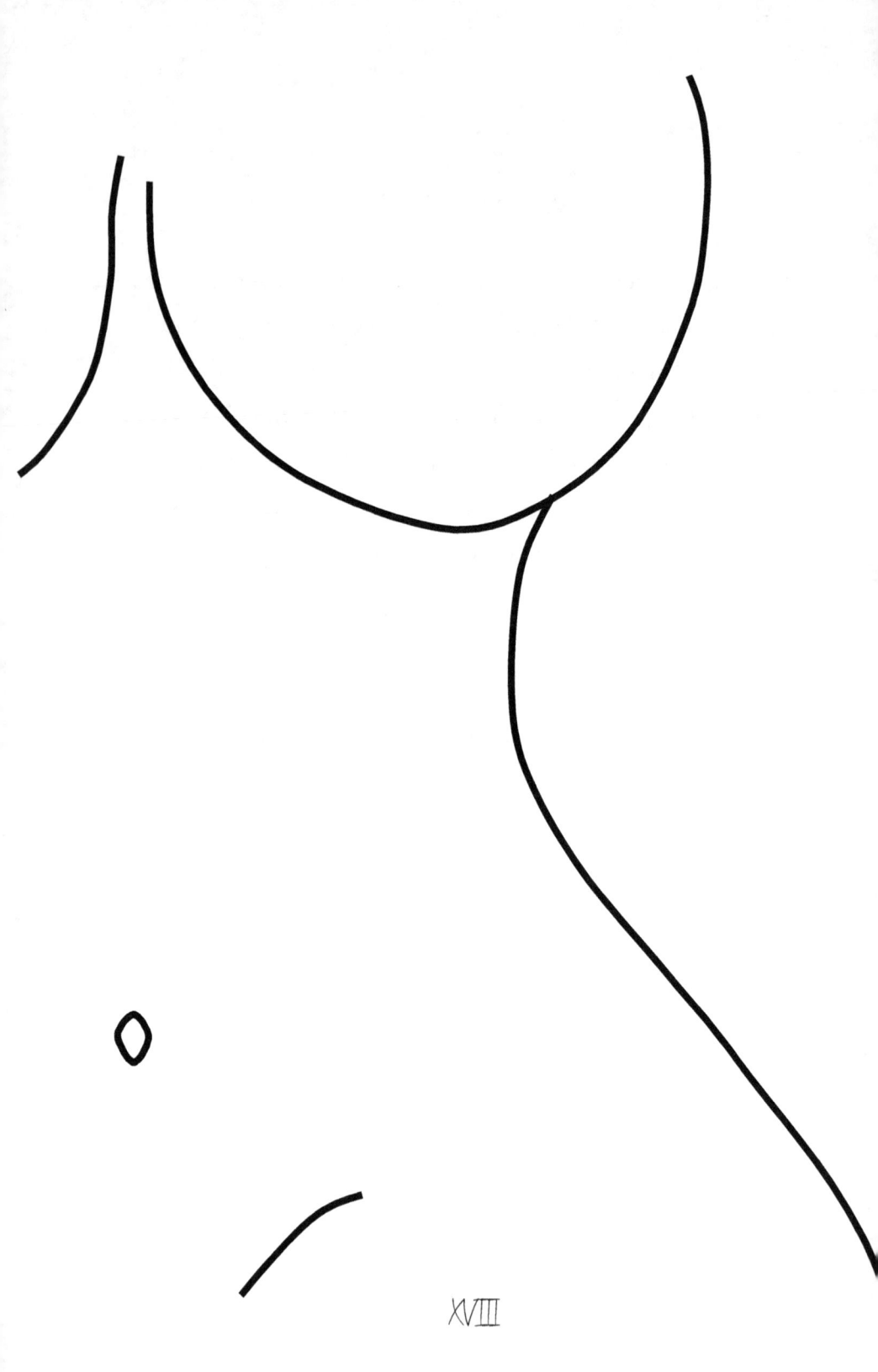

CHAPTER 1:

Silhouettes

Prayer

I pray for your strength and clarity
I pray for your courage and peace of mind
I pray on your worst days you make it look fucking amazing
I pray God lifts your feet when you feel heavy
And your head when you feel low
I pray you remember you are strong
You are beautiful
And you are special
I pray you know someone loves you
And when you feel like no one does
I pray you call me so I can tell you that I do.

Son (Takari)

You are the life that I created
My biggest blessing and greatest achievement
I promise to always protect you
Guide you and teach you

I love you

You are my heart in human form
You are the best parts of me
And the greatest parts of yourself
You help me stay sane
You are the universe's best creation

I love you more

You give me peace
You make my soul smile
You bring alive my inner child
And make my cup overflow
You make me whole

I love you the most.

Silhouette

I stand in the dark
My silhouette becomes art
My curves flow
Like the ocean's waves
Like the landscape

My mountains rise
With each breath I take
My river runs so fluidly
Slides and glides
My body speaks
So fluently

My silhouette becomes painted
On the canvas of my sheets
Beneath me
They sweep across
My soft skin

It's breathtaking
As the sea drifts
My hips shift
And open up
Like the inlets of a bay

My body sways
Like the winds of a hurricane
Destroying everything in its path
And I grasp
All the attention
With my silhouette.

Soulmate

You are passion
You are peace
You are love
And intimacy
I love you deep
From the bottom of my heart
To the deepest part of my soul
You make me fall

You are love
You are light
You ignite
The fire in my spirit
I can feel it
You speak life into me
And you make me want to be better

I surrender
To your power
I submit
As you lead
You breathe strength into me
And I can conquer the world

You are patient
You are serene
You are the calm to my storm
You protect and provide
You are my low and my high
And everything in between
You are my blessing
You make me glow
You are God's gift to me

The half
To my whole
The mate to my soul
And I am forever grateful.

Destined

I think I knew you in a past life
Like we're soulmates
And were made to fit just right

I think I loved you in an alternate universe
Like Miles and Gwen
In the Spider-verse

I think I met you on another planet
Like aliens in outer space
And both our ships were damaged

I think I needed you in a different time
Like Back to the Future
You know, Marty McFly

I think God saved you just for me
No matter the time or place or space
We were destined to be.

I Deserve Love

I deserve love

I am enough

I can provide
What I require

Beyond and above.

Second Chance

Like silhouettes hiding in the shadows
I've become shallow
I've turned selfish
I've felt it
For a while now

The changes that I've made
To save myself
Have inspired me
To love out loud

I no longer care for the hate
The secret animosity
I'm
Becoming beautiful again
And releasing the toxicity
No one can take that from me

I'm
Stepping into my power
Empowering myself
On this journey
Of love and light and wealth

The weapons that have formed
Shall never prosper
I've been offered
A second chance

I'm becoming alive
And no longer just living
The feeling is immaculate
And I've just scratched the surface.

Drunk Text

Drunken nights

I'm floatin'
I'm so high

I feel the waves of the ocean

I'm soakin'
Wet

So ready
To send this drunk text.

Turn It Up

You say I'm doing too much
You're not doing enough

So, there's that

As a matter of fact
Let me turn it up a notch

You don't like it?

You don't have to watch
Mute, block, unfollow
Pick one.

Happy Hour

I like my
Remy straight
Patron, no lime
Honey in my Jack
Moscato for my wine
Henny on the rocks
Pineapple in my Ciroc
Peach margaritas
Amaretto sour
Disarrono me please
This is my happy hour.

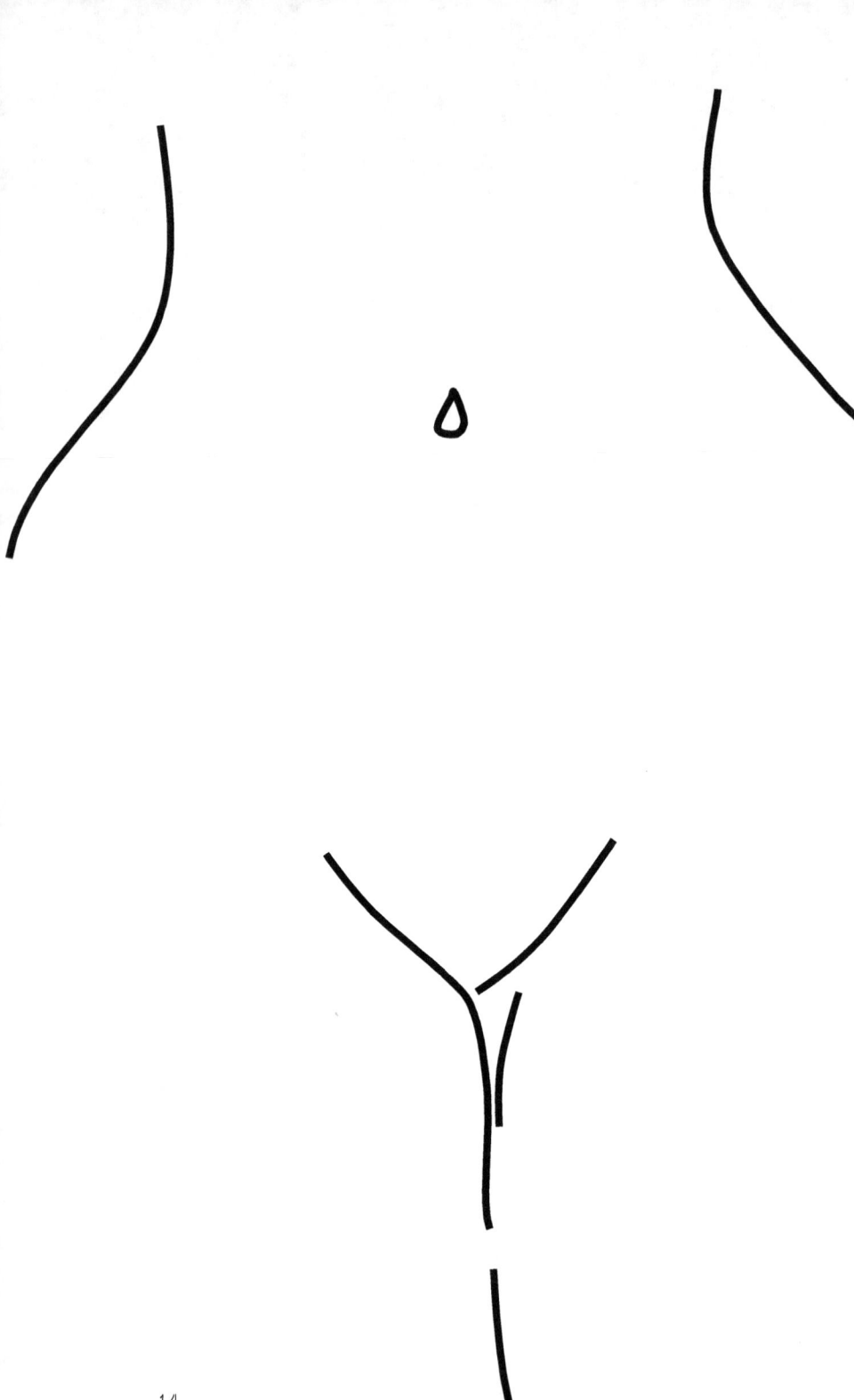

CHAPTER 2:

Sacrifices

The "Talking" Stage

Things turned
From something
To
Nothing
Real fast
Like
Whiplash

I'm
So confused
Feels like
I'm
Crashing
Into glass

These things
Never last.

Love language

What's your love language

Do you crave physical touch?
Is love displayed by how much
Your person hugs you
Kisses you
Caresses you
Undresses you

Do you need words of affirmation?
Verbal confirmation
Oral admiration
With no limitations
Simple conversations
That end in reassurance

Or is your love language
Acts of service?
Does love need to service you
By opening your door
Completing household chores
Breakfast in bed
To show that you deserve this

Maybe it's quality time
When he sets aside a few hours
For date night
Is that what makes you feel right
Is that the language that speaks to you?

Or do you need to be appeased
With gifts
Presents

To make his presence felt
Is that what makes your heart melt
Satisfies your soul
Diminishes your anguish

Tell me,
What's your love language?

Patient With Me

I'm impulsive sometimes
I have anxiety that causes me to need reassurance
I shut down when people speak to me a certain way
Please watch your tone.

I need consistency
I get you're not available all the time
But I would like it if you at least responded to my messages
Don't leave me on read
When my text is open ended.

I want to make this work
And see if it develops into something serious
I'm just afraid of getting hurt
And not getting my needs met.

But when you speak to me
And your tone is condescending
I shut down completely
When someone's behavior with me
Shifts drastically, suddenly
It triggers me.

Please be patient with me
I promise, it'll be worth it
We both deserve it
A relationship of reciprocation
That leads to a forever love.

You Give Me Butterflies

I trace your silhouette
As I stare at you in the dark
Recreating art
We fall apart
And then
Back together again

I surrender to your grasp
I gasp for air
As you take my breath away
I beg you to stay
With my lips pressed against yours
I feel you deep in my soul

You give me butterflies

I try to hide the feelings I lock inside
But they escape in time
And I become lost
In my thoughts of you

Thoughts of you
And me
And how 'we' can never be
But I will not leave

I will stay until you walk away
Even if you're bad for me
Even if you take my sanity

I will stay with you
As long as you let me.

The Kinda Love

I want the kinda love that
Sends me to the stars
Not that 'puts an ache in my heart' type love
That 'takes me to the moon and back'

As a matter of fact
I want the kinda love that
Heals me from the hurt of my past
That
Kinda love that touches my soul real fast
Not that
Half assed kinda love

The kinda love that
Hits you so hard, it
Makes you wonder who you are, and
How you ever got so far without it

The kinda love that
Puts me on a pedestal and
Puts himself right next to me
So that
Both of us are elevated
Both our love is understated
Underrated and integrated
And you never hesitated
To love me better...
More than ever

The kinda love that
Writes love letters, and
Draws hearts in the sand
The kinda love that

Is filled with romance
The kinda love between a woman and man
The kinda love that
Takes you by the hand into infinity
And beyond

The kinda love that's
Like a '90s R&B song
That Boyz II Men, Jodeci, Jagged Edge kinda love
That 112, Tyrese, Keith Sweat kinda love

My
Sweet lady
My
Peaches n cream
That
Let's get married kinda love
You know
The kinda love that
Lasts forever

The kinda love that
Got me twisted over you
Takes me to the end of the road with you
The kinda love that fights through
4 minutes like Avant
That's the kinda love that I want.

Love Showers

As I
Envision his kisses upon my lips, I
Can feel his fingertips drift
From my
Hips
My
Sensitive spots
Down to my
Inner most thoughts
It's like
He bought a book on how to love me
'Cause he sure knows how to love me

As he
Strokes the keys of my piano
See,
I know he can feel my body tremble
Like
The sound of a treble cleft
As he sets
My body on fire

The higher I go
The deeper I feel him enter my soul
Twisting and turning
We begin to flow
Into a sea of ecstasy

He
Comes into me
Then
Cums into me
Intimately

And
Sensually
We begin to make love showers

He devours
The best parts of me
Stroking my body
Like a melody of love

Leaving traces of his presence
On my senses
And once again
I sense his presence all over me

Thriving off my entire being
Making love to me ever so gently
Seductively
Entering my body
And passing through my dreams

Pretending to be
The man of my dreams
It seems
That
No one can compete
Because he
Is where I want to be

I'm
So intrigued by his physique
His
Unique ability to please me
So I
Need him
And I
Want him

So that
We can make love showers.

The One

The way that you hype me
Excites me
Ignites something inside me
I think you might be
The one

You
Make me better
Make me
Wetter
Make me
Wanna write you love letters

The way you love me
Makes me
Love you
The way you love me
Makes me
Love me

You
Hold me accountable
You
Bless me with consistency
You
Shower me with compliments
You
Just might be
The one

The way you
Cater to me
Acknowledge me

Inspire me
The way you
Favor me
Tend to me
Bring out my higher being

You seek to please me
Intentionally appease me
Effortlessly tease me
It brings me to my knees

You lead
And I submit
I'm convinced
That you're
The one.

Milk in His Coffee

My pretty pink toes
Against his full, sexy lips
As he slips
His tongue around them
He touches my skin
As he swims deep in my ocean
He's soaking wet
From my lucid depth
My fluids flow all over him

He kisses me slow
His hands glide below
And my body begins to shake
He looks deep in my eyes
I can feel him inside
As he grasps my neck and waist

Deep strokes
While he chokes me softly
Flips me over
We mix like milk in his coffee
His speed gets slower
His whole body's pressed against mine
He goes deeper
My legs get weaker
He slides his fingers down my spine

Our sweat combines
Bodies come alive
He's searching to find my spot
In and out
Up and down
Temperatures getting hot

Breathing gets heavy
Pace becomes unsteady
This feeling won't last forever
His grip gets harder
I'm dripping like water
We both cum together.

How to Love You

Teach me how to love you
Be patient with me
I have so much to give
There's an ache in me

Starving for love
Reaching for some kind of affection
Acceptance
Reciprocation
Without being left with nothing

I have a hard time trusting
Rushing
Into something
That becomes so meaningless
Seemingly
I'm trying this differently

Will you wait with me?

While I slowly let my guard down
I've found something in you
That makes me want to
But I need time
So that your heart can catch mine

I've seen the signs
They all lead to you
When you're ready
I'm ready
To learn how to love you.

Patiently

Thought about you today
Prayed
For your soul
I would sew
The pieces of your heart back to whole
If you would just let me get close

Let me let my guard down
And I will surround you
With everything you lost
When you thought you found love
You shove me into the friend zone
When I give you all things you need to feed your soul?

How do you not know?
Not see
All that we can be if you just set your past free

Scared to love
Because of a love you thought was love
Didn't love you back
She lacked
The qualities that would satisfy your deepest desires

But you're too blinded to look at me
Afraid that I will set fire to your flames
And you won't be able to tame
The feeling of feeling me
But I will wait, patiently.

Red Flags

He touched my soul
Gave me butterflies
Turned me blind to my intuition, I
Ignored my suspicions, I
Contradicted
Everything I stood by

I sat up at night
Wondering what his love was like, He
Touched the deepest parts of me

Intrigued me
Exceeded
Expectations
Of how a man was supposed to lead me
It's like he
Needed me
He was
Sweet to me
He treated me
Like we were meant to be

Obsessed with my lips
And my hips
As they would shift when I walked by
I was infatuated
With his face
I could taste
The Remy straight
When
He would say
"Bae"

He
Intoxicated me
And I fell in love

I
Craved his hugs
He became my drug
And
I don't even do drugs

I wasn't looking for love
Hell, I don't even like nobody
But, He
Felt like somebody
MY somebody
And I
Wanted to be his, I
Waited for his kiss, I
Wanted to be missed, I
Wanted him to be persistent
Consistent
Innocent
Literate
To my heart
To my soul
To my mind

I
Needed him to know
What my love felt like
So we could
Take flight
So we could
Feel right
So I could
Light
His soul on fire

The way he did mine

I didn't mind
His flaws, His
Red flags
That I probably shouldn't have ignored
But lorrddd
That man was fine
And I wanted so badly to call him mine.

No, Thank You

You went from
Double texting
To hours between messages

And green bubbles

See, the trouble is
I don't have time for the games
I don't like to play with people's time
So, when it comes to mine
I won't let you

I
Just met you
Why would I expect you
To play by my rules

You can get gone

I
Rather be
Left alone
Then to be
Dragged along

See I
Suffer from anxiety
And it
Makes me a little crazy
And I
Don't think you can handle that
Matter of fact
I don't even wanna be like that

So, I
Rather spend my time alone
Then to be led on
By some fool
Who thinks it's cool
To play with me

No, thank you.

You've Got a Hold on Me

I've been holding on to nothing
Something in my soul
Just won't let you go

You've got a hold on me

Lately
I've been seeing double
Seeing faces in places that don't belong, Like
Words in a song that don't rhyme, Like
Right place, wrong time, I've
Become blind

You've got a hold on me

An image of you keeps calling out to me
Misleading
Screaming
Bleeding

You've got a hold on me

I
Can't let go
It's like I
Lose control
And I
Start moving off emotion

I'm
Slowly approaching
The end of my rope
I'm

Sick of dealing with you
You
Pick and choose
When you wanna fuck with me
And I
Can't believe the audacity
But

You've got a hold on me.

First Time

I'm kinda nervous
This is my first time
So, I
Sip this wine to unwind
And ease my mind

I seem to find myself
Lost in a trance
It's as if your hands
Found their way to my favorite spot
And came across new seductions
Touched my emotions
And had me falling deep

You fell deeper
As I slowly slipped into a daze
Like I had been smoking on haze
And I don't even get high

But you had me flying passed the sky
Up into the stars
Our hearts began to melt together
And your words became a song

I got lost in the clouds
As I screamed your name out loud
My body trembled
And you smiled at the sound

My legs wrapped around your waist
As you raced through my soul
I felt us become whole
And then my body convulsed

I laid on top of you
As you laid in me
Stayed in me
Came in me
Effortlessly
As if we were meant to be
I was yours
And you were mine
It was my
First time.

We slept together last night
Fell asleep on the phone
I felt you next to me
But I was all alone

I missed your touch
And the feel of your kiss
But to hear you just breathe
I couldn't resist

We slept together last night
Fell asleep on the phone
Even though you weren't next to me
It felt like home.

Cupid

I keep going in circles
Trying to figure out how Cupid missed us

Completely skipped us
On his agenda to make us fall in love

Seems he lacks the aim to make the perfect match
And now he wants his arrows back

It's unfortunate

See, I've loved you since way before I knew you
But it took me so long to love you
And I let you love me way before you'll ever love me
It seems this match by Cupid was always doomed.

Remy Straight

He was
Better than sex
Better than drugs
He had me on my toes
Before we ever made love

He was sweet
Brown skin
Waves on swim
Beard was immaculate
He was passionate
Kissed me slow
He was handsome
Had me at "hello"

He gave me
Butterflies
Made me
Kinda shy
Made me
Feel so high
Like I'd been drinking all night

Slightly intoxicated
I was infatuated
He was my favorite
And I'd order him every time
He was my…
Remy straight.

For the Streets

Tweeting other bitches on Twitter
That shit makes me bitter
'Cause you left my messages on read

"But you can't get mad
Remember
We're not together"

But that's exactly what you said

Playing games with my heart
I gotta be on guard
Otherwise
I know you'll leave me scarred

I don't wanna be a part of this
He's clearly for the streets
But I'm too deep in
I've turned stupid
I thought we were playing for keeps

Because you pursued
And I alluded
To the fact
That I was attracted to you
Liking your pic
You know,
The one with your knees out
Little did I know
You'd have me wildin' out over you

I was
Overdue

For a rendezvous
But this ain't what I was looking for

I just
Liked your whore shorts
Had I known you were a whore
I would've left you alone

And now I lay here wondering
If you're even still interested
I don't wanna waste my time
After all, you ain't even mine.

Lipstick Stains

I sleep with my lips pressed against him
He awakens with my kiss
Fixed upon his cheek
Pretty in pink

My
Lipstick stains his skin
And he thinks...
Unique
And one of a kind
He knows it's mine
And I am his
From a distance
But still

The color paints a pretty picture in my head
Of a time when he and I will be intertwined
Beneath a sky of
Silver stars and twinkling lights
And she is out of the picture

Like a scripture
Our fate will be written
And our destiny fixed
Like his eyes on my hips
As they shift
And switch positions
Making him fall deeper and deeper
Into me

You see
He and I are meant to be
And she will eventually

Be erased from his memory
Especially
When she finds his tee
With traces of my lipstick stains.

The Other Woman

Okay
So here I go
Here I go again

Sending myself
Through a whirlwind of emotion
Trying to figure out where he's been

His tired lies
And loss of track of time
Got me in a bind with my heart and mind
I surely denied
All the things I saw
Acted like
I never witnessed them at all
But her face
Just won't erase
From the center of my brain

See, she was the one that he pictured
Every time he made love to me
And when his phone would ring
He'd be hoping it was her

The way things were
I just couldn't save us
His lust
Must have turned into love
And left me
Drowning in a pool of my own tears

He would not rescue me
But instead

Threw her the life jacket
So, I swam until I ran out of breath
And slowly sank to the bottom
While she crept her way back up
To take my spot

Now they live happily ever after
And I'm waiting for my turn
Waiting for my king
And my fairy tale ending

When I can stop pretending
That I no longer hurt
From the worst type of pain
When I can confidently say
...I'm over u.

Am I?

I still think of you when you're not around
Still
Wonder if you'd put it down if I called
Still
Ponder if I'm on your mind for any reason whatsoever

Am I?

Can I
Come over and see you?
Maybe
Give it to you
For an hour or two

Possibly put my lips against your lips
As my body
Slips
Up and down, over yours

Do you fantasize about the way I ride?
About how good you used to feel inside me?
The way I used to roll my tongue around yours
What about when I used to....
Never mind
That's too explicit

You just crossed my mind
And the time
We used to spend
Loving one another
The few hours that were so full of pleasure
I fell deeper every time you fell deeper

Whenever you called
I came
And whenever I called your name
You came

I miss you coming
I miss how aroused you would get
From just touching me
I miss you touching me
So, can I
Come see you?
Just for an hour or two
So I can leave traces of my presence all over your skin?

Will you let me in
Just one last time?
So I can leave a lasting impression
On your mind

I promise it will be worth it
And in the morning, I'll text you two little words
Just to help you rise and shine

Am I?

It's Over

I was trying not to break
But you broke me
Destroyed me
Disturbed my peace
Until the pieces no longer fit together
I thought we were forever

You became ugly and mean
When you said you meant no harm
You left me with scars
Took my heart
And ripped it apart
What I thought was the start
Of something so beautiful
Turned into chaos and regret

You set me up for a downfall
Now I'm spiraling out of control
And I can't see the end of the tunnel

Save me
From the hurt that you gave me
You blame me
For the flaws in our relationship
I can't sit with this

It's over.

Raw

My love was too raw
Like no rubbers
And no covers
No protection
No contraception
Just flesh on flesh
Searching for connection

Our interactions
Were so natural
Casual
But factual
Caught up in lust
I took you as you were

Opposites attracted
Causing negative reactions
Two broken hearts
And we're back to where we started
We never made it very far
I love too hard
But I'm also hard to love

Starving for physical touch
And emotional hugs
I began to lose myself in you
I let you control the narrative
An abusive comparison
Stuck between the two

Our story was
Rough drafts
And failed pasts

Torn pages out of a book
It was disaster at first sight
Scared to make it right
Or even take a second look

Our love was too raw
But moved too fast
Bound to crash
Running into dead ends
We wanted it so bad
But turned so sad
Knowing it wasn't meant to be

I couldn't see
The pain you were causing me
I was too busy loving you
I was so intrigued
By your abilities
And how our passion grew

But my love was too raw
Like no rubbers
And no covers
No common sense
To relieve the tension
Just flesh on flesh
Waiting for ascension.

Love him

So I'm like
Diggin' this dude
That doesn't even notice me
Seems to be me focusing
Too hard on the obvious

He's
Obviously not into me
But he plays as if he craves me

In all actuality
He knows
In reality
That I'm
Obsessed with his ability
To make me love him

So intrigued with his style and demeanor
The way he's meaner
To these hoes

He makes me stare
Until he
Catches me
Falling completely

But I cave under the pressure
Of his
Intellectual
He's oh so sexual
And at the same time
Delectable

I want to taste his thoughts
And grasp his sexy conversations

See,
I've been waiting
For the day and the time
That he's finally mine
And we will forever be part of one another
Whether
Under the covers or
On top of the sheets
He
Will be with me
Making love to my mind
Robbing me blind
Of the peaceful state of mind
I once was in

And
If loving him is sinful
Then the devil is a liar
And God will forgive me

Because the love he gives me
Is so divine
That it will open the gates of heaven
And let me in
And then, again
I will be able to love him.

Never Lasts

So in love
With being in love
That my love
Turned into nothing

Underestimated
And
Overrated
Taken so lightly
That
It blinded me
From seeing
Just where I needed to be

He
Gave me butterflies
And teary eyes
That I'd try to hide
But
In the meantime
He was on a path of destruction

Knowing the direction
In which he reflected
I got left behind

Thinking I'd find
A feeling of some kind
That would
Make me feel brand new

That he could undo
All the pain from my past

And this time it would last

With no regrets
I opened my heart

To the same type of guy
That made me cry
Time and time again
Burying my pain
In the validity that
He made me feel

Trusting what I thought was real
Sealing a deal with the de'vil
...I mean, devil

Now
A rebel against love
Against losing pieces of my heart
When he
Breaks it completely apart

Like smashed art
And broken glass
I'll never understand
Why it didn't last.

Untitled

He's slowly flowing
Through my every motion
Like lotion on my skin
He's created a potion out of sin
Making me wonder where he's been

Sipping on my juices
He seduces and reproduces
Reaching into my soul
Giving me feelings that I don't wanna feel again

Sheltering my emotions with a force field
He's superhuman
Got me going dumb
I'm suffering from stupid
Fiending for his love
He's like a drug
And I'm addicted
Forget shot
I've been killed by cupid

I wanna hate him
But that line is too thin
I just can't win going up against him

He's got me seeing stars, and
Drawing hearts around our names
He took me from insane
To totally crazy in the membrane
That I couldn't possibly see things the same

My mind frame
Has completely changed

With old endings
And new beginnings

I'm treading water
Trying to avoid drowning
In a pool full of kid games
Such a shame

He's mentally challenging
And I'm mentally challenged
When it comes to him
He should be illegal
The way he's got me going

He's amazing
Also stimulating
Multi-talented
The way he has my body imitating
The signs of a seizure

As he goes deeper
My mind becomes weaker
My heartbeat, a speaker
I emulate an alcoholic drinker
Think I need AA

Better yet eight days away from him
That's how long before I begin
To have withdrawals

These four walls begin to close in
On my ability to stay sober

I'm over
The fact that we can't be together
But I need to have you as my lover

See rehab is just kinda sad
And I don't think I belong there
My addiction is controllable
As long as it's not noticeable
That I need it

So as long as you supply
And I forcibly try
To not get caught up in my mind
I will be alright

'Cause this fight against him
I don't think I'll ever win.

Fantasy

I go to sleep and dream my fantasies
How you make love to me
When you kiss me in places
That hide so easily

Touch every inch of me
Dive deep
Come into me
Then
Cum into me

Take all of me
And give me everything
Every ounce
Of your very being

Slip beneath me
As I come over you
Make me cum all over you
Do it 'til I scream your name
Then do it again
And again
And again

Fill me up with your love
Then love me 'til the sun comes up
Give it to me
Like it's the first time

Fuck me like you need me
Make my heavy breathing
I mean, breathing heavy
See how fantasizing got me unsteady

Got me seeing stars
But you're so far
And I need it
So, you will be my fantasy
Until I can have it.

CHAPTER 3:

Sabotage

Still Birth

Beep…beep..beep

The IV machine is beeping again
I'm lying in this hospital bed
Waiting for my unborn child
To be born dead

Planning her funeral before her birth
God,
Do you understand the kind of hurt you're putting us through?

This is crazy

My mind ain't right
I'm all confused
Beating myself up
I don't know what to do

Labor pains
Emotionally drained
I feel like I'm going insane

Hands bruised
Turning black and blue from this IV tube
Medication's flowing into my veins
As I'm delivering my beautiful baby in vain

Lord,
Give her life again
Please,
Give her life again!

For my daughter,
Takai Semaj Ilus
10.22.2009

Suicide Attempts

She hates her life
Figures it'd be easier for her to die
Because living is too hard

She takes the knife
But can't seem to push through
Maybe pills
An overdose would do
She empties the bottle
Chases it with wine
She passes out in no time
But the dosage of the medication
Was too low
Her blood flow slowed
But she was still alive
Worst hangover ever

Once she's sober
She finds a revolver
Puts it to her head
But she can't find the strength
To pull the trigger
Go figure

She hates being alive
But it's becoming clear
That it's too hard to die
She gives it one more try

She ties the noose
Hangs it from the roof
Slips it on
And in minutes

She's gone.

For Ma
2.26.1962-9.2.2019

Myself

For months I wasn't myself
I felt ugly inside and out
I couldn't look in the mirror
Without wanting to cry

I smiled through the pain

Too ashamed
To express the way I was really feeling
So, I covered it up
With my Mac concealer
And my makeup brush

Saint Germain on my lips
So my kiss would still taste as sweet
Whole time I couldn't defeat
The demons deep within me
Fighting against them, as I
Swallowed the bitter bites of my life
Overwhelmed by the ache in my soul
I was no longer whole
I was a piece of what began to feel like nothing

I felt so alone
So unknown
And in the midst of my depression
I became so lost
Calculating the cost
Of getting my life back
Finding myself in the chaos
Making sure my L wasn't a loss
But rather a lesson

Praying for my blessing
So that I could rise from the fire
Emerge from the sorrow
That I began to wallow in
Wondering if I'd ever be myself again.

Rain

Against my windowpane, I
I can't stand the rain
Because it hides my pain
A pain that I want to feel
So that I can finally heal

But the rain, rain
Won't go away
Won't let me stay in my misery
Misery loves company and she accompanies me
Through my hurt and my grief
I lay in disbelief
That she could take this from me

Rain, rain
Don't you see
I need to be left alone

Knocking sounds
Pound in my head
Again, and again
Noise and pain blend into a sea of chaos The
rain drops…drop
Filling a pool of sorrow

I can't wait until tomorrow
When it will be sunny again

See
The sun
She gets me
She lets me
Live in my misery

She
Understands
That if I don't face my demons
I can never get passed this
Never move on
Never grow
Or be whole
Again

But the rain, rain
Just won't let me win
Won't let me have my day in the shade
I mean, sun

That's it
I'm done
I'm going inside
'Cause

This rain, rain
Won't go away.

You Don't Wanna Love Me

You don't wanna love me

I'm so broken
I come with a ton of baggage
A broken heart and enough grief
It would take too much effort for you to 'see' me
You could never comprehend what it takes to be me
You see
I've been damaged
Beat down and betrayed
Emotionally scarred and enslaved
Mentally drained
Abandoned
And I've become somewhat deranged
You don't wanna love me

I'm incapable of loving you back
My heart is packed with ugly scars and has been torn apart
I don't know if there's a way back for me
You don't wanna love me

You think I'm pretty
But these looks have become only skin deep
When I look in the mirror, I don't even recognize me
I dwell on what could be
Would be
Should be
You don't wanna love me

I've been hurt, abused, and left for dead
Maybe it's all in my head
But the shit I've been through is enough to kill you

Enough to drive you far away from me
You don't wanna love me

No second thoughts, you
Couldn't afford the cost
The things I've lost took a piece of me
Chipping away at my whole
Now this hole is left here
Where my heart once was
So, when I say there's no love here
I mean it

Just because you can't see it
Doesn't mean it doesn't exist
This pain that sits on my chest
It's enough to drive you to slit your wrists
Thoughts of suicide
Thoughts you'd try to hide
Because no one would believe
You'd take your own life

I get so lonely
So empty
If only you could see why

You don't wanna love me.

Breaking Point

I had reached a new low
My breaking point
My spirit was tainted
And my soul undone
I started feeling like
The trauma I encountered had won

I slowly slipped into a black hole of emotion
The commotion it caused inside of me
Sent me into a sea of emptiness
Relentlessly
Pulling me deeper and deeper
I've reached my breaking point

The people around me became distant shadows
As I disconnected and no one followed
The anxiety attacks got worse
And the outbursts...
I should've warned them first.
I didn't want them to think I was crazy
But my overthinking set in
And I began to push everyone away
Not realizing
I was only hurting myself
My selfish ways began to weigh on me
I was at my breaking point

I was braking
Because I was broken
I couldn't take it
I left so many things unspoken
Unsaid
Felt like I had been left for dead

But it was me
Drowning in self-pity
I was passed my breaking point

It was time to heal.

Was It Worth It?

Did it hurt?
Was it worth it?
Are you sure?

Did you enjoy watching me bleed
All over the floor
When I poured
My heart out to you?

Did it pain you
When you beat my soul
Black and blue?

Was it fun
When you took my love for granted?
Did you like
Taking advantage of me?

Were you nervous
When you lied?
Did you smile
When I cried?

All bullshit aside,
Was it worth it?

What If

I'm scared to let you love me
That gives you access to leave me
Deceive me,
Mistreat me,
Believe me,
I've tried

I've cried my share of tears
So now I give in to my fears
Of loving someone too much
Not giving him a chance to see the real me
To feel me,
To love me,
Properly

The "what ifs" kill me
Destroy every opportunity
To be happy
I'm tired

If I open myself up to love
What if you switch up?
What if I'm not enough?
What if you don't love me back?
What if I lack
All the qualities you look for
What if you need more
Than I can give
Or vice versa
What if I hurt you
Or you, me

See

That's what I'm afraid of
It isn't love that scares me
It's the "what ifs".

Learning to Love

I don't know how to love
I don't know how to not hold back
I lack the ability
To show you my real feelings

I've been exposed in the past
Vulnerable
Caused me to be taken advantage of
Shut down for being myself
So now I hide

I could never express
How I really felt
Without being pushed to the side
Fear has set in
The trauma of the drama
That being honest created

Feelings faded
Habits traded
So now instead of being soft
My wall is up
And I'm stuck being hard

Hiding my scars
Trying not to fall apart
Because I love so hard
My feelings take control
And I lose my focus

It's hopeless
I'm open
To allowing love in

But I don't want to be hurt again.

'Til Death

Seems like time has slowed down
And then stopped
My heart has dropped
Into the pit of my stomach
And has yet to resurface

The more I try to control my emotions
The more I cry from being so broken

The hands on my clock no longer tick
Yet the years have flown by
Turning you into just a memory

I pray every night
For you to come visit
But you said your goodbye
And I haven't seen you since

I ask God for just a moment
A small piece of a conversation
Maybe just a glimpse of your face
Outside of my imagination
But you never come

Lost in my thoughts
I reminisce about us
And time nor death
Could ever erase or replace you in my heart

So instead of 'til death do us part
We are now 'til death do us reunite
'Cause once I take flight
And God calls my soul home

I know, you and I
Will once again, be one.

For Reggie.
12.23.1985-8.19.2009

Loss for Words

Wish I had a shot of you
To make me feel just right

I would
Take flight
Off the feeling of flying

Feels like I'm dying
'Cause I'm trying
So hard to enjoy it

I'm a poet
At a loss for words
All the words I write
Seem to start off right
And turn so left
Since you left

I meant to say wrong
But it's like I said
I can't get the words right

I start off in love
But it turns into hate about eight bars in
I can't seem to win
'Cause every poem ends up about the same thing

It's amazing
And sickening
At the same time

Every time I start to rhyme
I force myself to stop

'Cause I'm so sick of trying
To come up with words that rhyme with you
"You damn fool
I'm tired of you too
And all the things you do
The shit you put me through
And the perfect picture you drew"

See what I mean
It just doesn't even sound good anymore

Like
The floor is shaking beneath me
And I'm losing my balance
'Cause with all this talent,
I just can't get it right.

Tainted

Your name is engraved
On my brain
It will forever remain
The source of my pain
And as I try to contain myself
From going insane
You put a strain on my soul

You spin me out of control
Then call me crazy

Our love was sweet
Like champagne
Smooth like Alizé
Unique, in its own way

But now
A drink is just a drink
And our glass is empty

My mind is tainted
From the paintings of a fabrication that you created
Time wasted
And energy spent
On something that was never meant to be

You see,
I could never be
Who you wanted me to be
You tried to change me
Enslave me,
Save me,
From the image you hated

You made it
So that I wouldn't love myself
Because you didn't love me

But now I am free
Of your hatred
And I can finally walk away
Knowing
That it was you
Who was tainted.

Slipping Away

I need to get out of my own head
I put the paper to the pen
And write my life away

Some days
I feel like a castaway
Need something to take this pain away

Help me fade
Into the darkness of my own mind
Fearful of what I might find
Time is not on my side

I've become blinded
By my traumas
I'm not a fan of drama
But I seem to always bring it

I think I need it
To feel something
Because my days are filled with nothing
And I'm slowly slipping away.

Self-Destructive

I'm self-destructive
Unproductive
Trapped inside my head
It's deconstructive

I'm overwhelmed with negativity
Insecurities
Bad vibes
And undesirable energy

I pray for peace and clarity
I pray for someone to see me
In need of uplifting
Seeking
My higher being

I'm losing myself
Losing my sanity
I'm slowly isolating
Removing people from around me

It's draining
And I'm exhausted
I think I've lost it
The cost is
Too expensive

I'm apprehensive
My behavior is
Reprehensible
I'm regressing
And it's destroying me

I'm self-destructive.

Self-Sabotage

He's been fighting demons
I've offered what I can
And he continues to push back
So, I left it at "ok"

I felt myself pouring too much
And I had to stop
He's self-sabotaging right now
He acknowledged that
Also said he has too much on his plate
Which I've stated before

Some people don't want to be saved
And you have to let them ruin themselves
So, I checked in
And as soon as I felt an ounce of being overwhelmed,
I checked out

Self-sabotage will cause you to miss your blessings
In those who were genuinely sent to help you heal
It feels
Like you want to wallow in your pain
And I cannot condone that

I do not condemn you for your choices
We all have to make them
But I refuse to enable the exact behavior
That has ruined me in the past

The pain doesn't last
Unless you let it
You don't get it
You have to set it free

So you can find peace
And be happy
You have to stop
Self-sabotaging.

Discernment

I have so much love to give
But I'm so negative
And I don't feel like I'm worthy

My thoughts wander
To the worst scenario
And I know that they don't serve me

But when I see the signs
Repeated patterns
I tell myself he doesn't deserve me

I think it's my mind
Playing tricks on me
And I no longer trust my discernment.

Toxic

I'm traumatized
I've sacrificed and compromised
Rationalized and have become paralyzed
I'm so tired

It's exhausting
Carrying this baggage
And I am in no position
To ask you to bear it

Would you care if
It ruined our relationship
I don't want to share
This burden with you

So, I exclude myself
From feeling the emotions
That may rock the boat
I just wanna float with you
But I can't bring myself
To fall in love with you

You see,
I'd rather be alone
With my pain
Than to drag you along
Through my reign

Save yourself the trouble, I
Live in this bubble
To keep myself sane
To isolate my pain
And to drown in the rain,

Alone

It's become home
And no visitors allowed

I can't love you out loud
Because the sound
Will drown out my misery
I don't wanna be
The one to hurt you, but I
Can't let go of this hurt
It's too much work
I'd be losing too much of myself
All the ugliness
I've become so comfortable with
It will cause a shift
In my balance
And that doesn't work for me

It would be too hard
To learn how to function without it
I've become toxic
And I fear
That by healing
I won't know who I am

Starting all over again
Doesn't seem ideal
It would be unreal
Unrealistic
To move past this
And become a new me
So, I'll stay here
Trapped in my toxicity.

Insensitive

How can you make me feel bad for giving a fuck?
How can you be so insensitive?
To someone who's being so sensitive to your needs
Someone who's willing
To let you bleed all over them
Willing to help you clean
The mess you created for yourself

You clearly don't want help
You project your pain
So that it's felt by others
You want them to suffer
From your own struggle
I won't be a crutch

You've become rude
And cold
Distant and bold
And you've begun to make me feel small

You're building a wall
And blocking me out
I'm there when it counts
But you've got one time
To make me feel like a burden
And I won't ever bother you again

I've sent
Thoughtful messages
And healing energy
And you just don't want it from me
And that's okay
But you cannot expect me to stay

When you continue to push me so far away
Then you complain that no one genuinely cares
So, I'll give you your space
But I cannot guarantee
I'll be here when you get back

Your lack of self-awareness
Has become weary
And I don't want any parts

To protect my heart
I have to step back

But I pray for your peace
I pray you find whatever it is
That you lack
Whatever it is
That you need.

Triggered

Shots fired
I'm triggered
I'm bleeding all over you
And you don't understand why
I start to cry
The pain has taken over
And you are lost in the chaos
Of my anxiety

You wait
For the overflow of emotions to subside
I'm trying to control it
But I'm slowly dying inside

The panic has taken over
There's no way I'm sober
And this out of control
You try to save me
But the racing in my mind
Has led me to believe
That you've betrayed me
I can't stay here

The faster I move
The more I begin to lose focus
The room is spinning
And you're too oblivious to notice

I'm not sure if
I've ever explained
The pain I experience
When I take something serious
And things begin to go wrong

I'm not strong enough to hold on
I'm not stable enough to shake this off
I need help

I'm drowning in a pool
Of my own plight
And there's no life raft in sight
I might just lose myself
In the waves of my depression
It would lessen the blow
If you just left me alone
And saved yourself

I won't
Guilt you into staying
Or manipulate you by saying
All the things you put me through
The feeling is mutual

If you leave
I will let you
I've been suffering since I met you
So, it's best if you go
You don't have to love me anymore
I know I've become too much

I've had such bad luck
Coping with my fuck ups
I wouldn't even blame you for going
But don't leave without knowing
Just how much I cared

I swear
I'll always be there
But right now, I figure
You should leave me
While I heal from my triggers.

Surviving

Lost my daddy at 13
Searched for him in the men I'd meet
Yes, I have daddy issues

Molested at 16
Almost raped at 19
This triggered my hyper-sexuality

My first love was killed at 23
Lost my daughter 2 months later
She died inside me

Pregnant again at 24
My son was 6 weeks premature
Lived in the hospital for months
While he fought for his life

2015 my brother committed suicide
I didn't even get to say good-bye
That's when my anxiety started

4 years later
I found my mother hanged in the backyard
I tried to save her
Performed CPR
Until she turned from pale to purple
I thought I could turn back time

2020 the pandemic hit
I sold my childhood home
And moved 250 miles away

I struggle everyday

To heal from the hurt of my past
A hurt that seems everlasting
Everyday I'm trying
Sometimes I wonder how I'm surviving.

Smashed Art

Like smashed art
I've destroyed a masterpiece
Disturbed the peace and left it in pieces

It never ceases to amaze me
How crazy
I can be when triggered
I figured
I'd be over this by now
But somehow
I'm still angry
Still hurt
And deceived

I've achieved nothing by staying here
I still live in fear
That it'll happen again
And I send you off into the chaos
Of my emotions

I was hoping
That I could've left it in the past
That it
Wouldn't last
But
The feelings never passed
And I'm not satisfied

I dry my eyes
From all the tears I've cried over this
I'm so tired and sick
Of the shit I've witnessed
And I need an escape

If you can't take it anymore
No longer want to endure
The effects of my insanity
I will let you go, sadly
But I know you need to leave
And put the pieces back together

I can never repair
The despair in my heart
It's destroyed
Like smashed art.

Send Nudes

"What you got on"
"Lemme see"
I'll never understand
Where you got the audacity
It must've been on sale.

You care more about the visuals of my body
Than to even ask me
How I'm doing.

It's really not that hard
To let the conversation get that far
Without you asking me.
I get that your imagining
What it looks like, actually
But let it happen, naturally.

Now, sometimes I don't mind
'Cause even though I'm kinda shy
When I send them
You hype me.

But when every conversation
Turns to wanting to see me naked
That's where I draw the line.
You never even took the time
To see what's on my mind
Maybe I'm going through some shit.

But that never hit you
And here you are again
Asking me to
Send nudes.

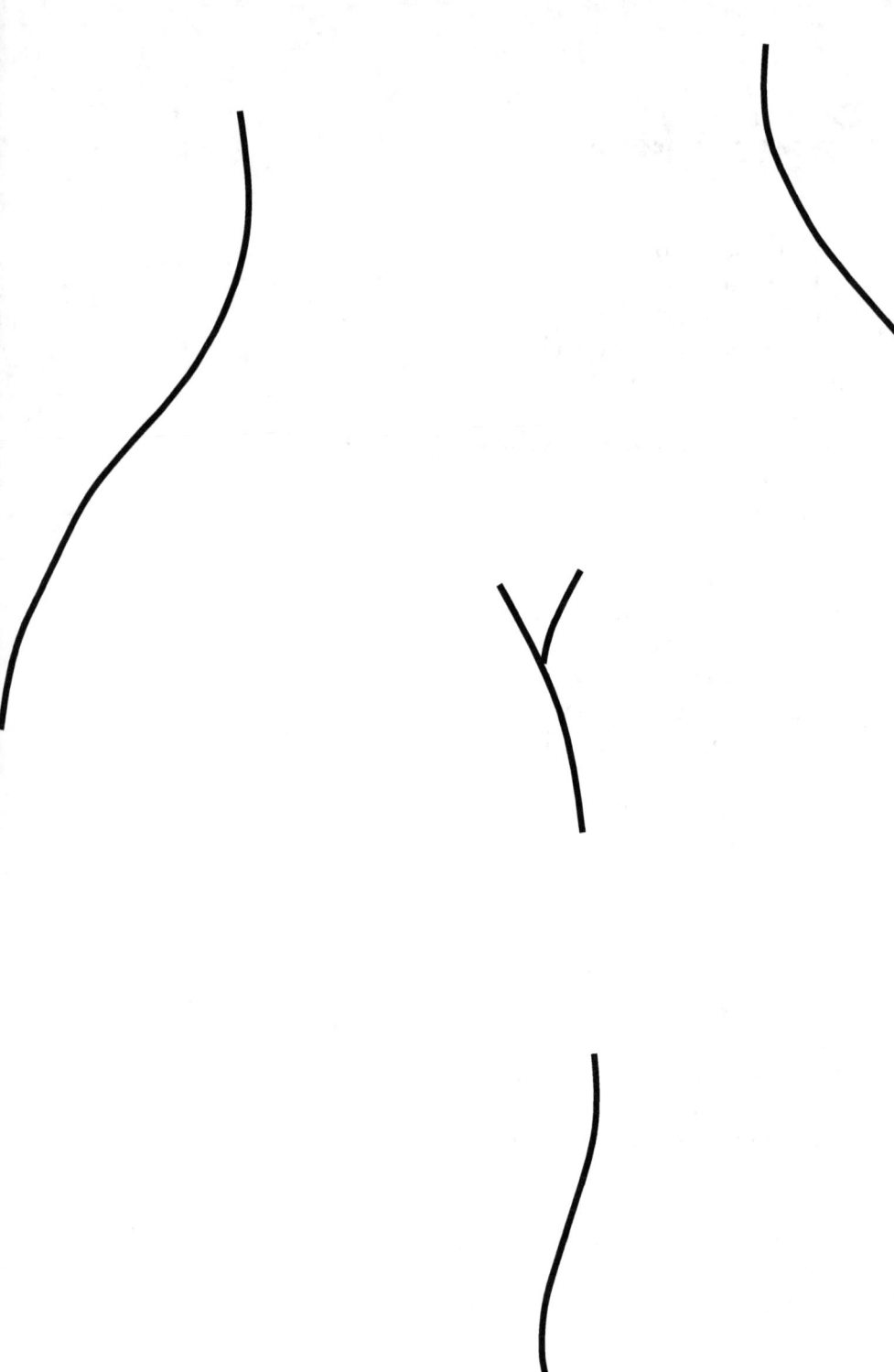

CHAPTER 4:

Soul

Flower

She begins to wilt away
Like the sun rays no longer shine on her face
As if she were a flower and life devoured her roots
Damaged her leaves
And burned out her petals

She became unsettled in the pot in which she was becoming old
Her stories untold
Longing for a new beginning
Heading for the end of the cycle of her life
And all the madness was soon to suffice

Once again
Leaving her cold and alone
To wilt away in the meadow of her soul.

Irrelevant

Distracted

By the fact that
You were so attractive
I began to indulge in the feelings
That I told myself I would not feel again

Trapped in suspense
On the edge of my seat
Like a horrible movie

The time I spent on worthless lies
And untold truths
Of how you used my love for you against me

I became weak

Every time you got on your knees
Thinking I was special
You got in my mental
And my physical
And my emotions
You got the best of me

Left me with the worst of myself
Living in hell with my heart on my sleeve
Now so deep in my soul
No man will ever know how to find it

You destroyed me with your selfish ways
And unselfish deceit
I cried myself to sleep

I refuse to shed tears for another man
That holds no regard
For my fears of being heartbroken

The words left unspoken
Can remain unsaid
And you
Can go to hell

'Cause when I fell
I landed on rocks
And now, bruised and bleeding
I'm getting back up
And I'm on the road to recovery

Even if that means
I gotta check myself into a facility
I'll be safe
And you can no longer hurt me

I will regain stability
And love me so unconditionally
That what you've done
Will be irrelevant.

Words for Thought

Rough times
Sacrifice
Try to survive
And keep your mind right

Inhale
Exhale
Prevail
With detail

Come correct
It's yours to protect
Never let them disrespect
Advance your intellect

Keep it real
Show how you feel
Announce the deal
Add sex appeal

Drown them out
Never doubt
Know what it's about
Consider the amount

Unwind
Spend time
Decline
Rewind

Participate
Don't hesitate
Infatuate

Overestimate

Obsess
Confess
Caress
Impress

Be wrong
Keep it on
Make it long
Be gone

Implicate
Complicate
Separate
Eliminate

Get yours
Be sure
Endure
Be secure

Don't get caught
Do it a lot
Don' be bought
Words for thought.

Talent

I can paint harmonies
Design melodies
Play poetry
And draw a song

I can write an improvisation
Off the top of my head
I can sing a movie
And dance a monologue

I can
Build a beat
Bang a lyrical
Walk a musical
And speak a comedy

I can
Laugh up a drama
And cry an action
Hate a romance
And live a horror

Act out oratorical
Dress a speech
Debate a fantasy
With the best quality

I can
Run a tune
Hold my balance
Do everything
With only talent.

Elevate

Fly by night
Let's take flight
Push me to new heights
Elevate me.

Epitome of a Gentleman

Accountability
Consistency
Persistency
Intrigue me

Effort
Transparency
Integrity
Fascinate me

Honesty
Spirituality
Trustworthy
Excite me

Maturity
Serenity
Masculinity
Entice me

Your ability
To inspire me
The way
That you desire me

The qualities
You possess
Make me
Completely obsessed

You lead
And I submit
You are the epitome

Of a gentleman.

Save You

I can only love you if you let me
You can't expect me
To fight for you
Without you inviting me to

I want to save you
But I can't
Without your consent

Everyone is not meant to be saved
Sometimes
You have to let people hit rock bottom
Maybe it's tough love
But how can I help
If you shut me out

I want to love you
But you can barely love yourself
I won't leave you
But I can only do so much
Without your trust
That I'm genuinely on your side

You hide your pain
But I want to see all your scars
Open up your heart
Let me in
Let me love you
Let me save you.

Transition

The fear of losing people
Has caused me to adopt toxic behaviors
I exhibit traits that are unfavorable
I fear being vulnerable
Approachable
Lovable
I have abandonment issues

I'm scared to share this with you
I've become comfortable
With my defense mechanisms
My trauma responses
That I no longer acknowledge
When they are triggered

It's easier to ignore
Than to admit when I'm torn
Between my emotions and my logic

I thought if
I explained why I am this way
Maybe you'd understand
Maybe
Hold my hand
Through my transition
My process to overcome
To change what I've become
To heal from my pain
And submerge in love and light again.

Stars Align

Deciding that my past traumas
Are not worth sacrificing my future over
I'm over
How much I let my pain
Get in the way
Of who I am made to be

Intentionally
I'm choosing positivity
Healing
And trusting my ability
To overcome
Negative feelings
And emotions

I'm hoping
To defeat my demons
And realize the dreams
I have are worth achieving

I'm seeing the stars align
And I know it's my time
To start living
And not just staying alive.

Pour Into You

I can no longer pour into those
Who do not pour into me
How are you okay with draining me
But not filling me back up
When I'm in need

You leave me on empty
And expect me to overflow your energy
It doesn't work like that

When you lack
I add
But when I lack
You subtract

How can I provide what you need
But you can't do the same for me
I struggle too

My batteries get used
The same way yours do
But I pour into you
And you let me

When it was time to reciprocate
You left me
I support and I endure
And you take
And then you take some more

So, I can no longer
Pour into you.

Let Go

I've come to the realization
That we don't want to let go of our pain
Because
It feels like we are forgetting the people that caused it
Or
The people we lost
Or
We've become so used to the pain that
We fear we won't know how to function without it

I am searching for peace
Love and serenity
And if I don't release
What's hurting me
I'll never heal

I am letting go of what was
I send it off
With love
And I step into the light
I let it shine
Brightly
On my skin
And into my soul
Today
I let go.